There's a WINNER in YOU

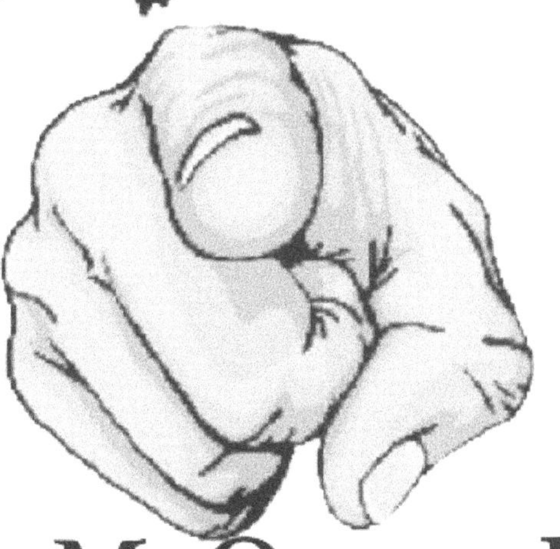

Marvin McQueen II

"There Is A Winner In YOU!"

By

Marvin A. McQueen II

© By Marvin McQueen II

All rights reserved. No part of this publication may be reproduced, distributed, or transmitted in any form or by any means, including photocopying, recording, or other electronic or mechanical methods, without the prior written permission of the publisher, except in the case of brief quotations embodied in critical reviews and certain other noncommercial uses permitted by copyright law. The uses of the short quotes or quotations are for personal growth from great-quotes.com and are permitted and encouraged. For permission requests, write to the publisher at www.marvinmcqueen2.com.

ISBN: 978-0-578-07403-0

Printed in the United States

This is to ALL of the WINNERS!!!

I thank my awesome father and mother,
Dr. Marvin and Kathy McQueen I.
I will always appreciate your foundation of teaching and your unconditional love.

We Are Winners!

Wanted:

Victims, Stressed People, Discouraged, Poor, Rich, Real People, Hurt People, Fearful People, Tired People, Unhappy, Sad, Happy, Mad, Angry, Excited, Girls, Boys, Men, Women, Loved, Unloved, Friends, Enemy, Professionals, Uneducated, College Students, Ethical, Generous, Intelligent, Honest, Creative, Trustworthy, Gorgeous, Bound, Ambitious, Brave, Alluring, Fun, Precious, Genuine, Thoughtful, Keen, Forceful, Energetic, Incredible, Marvelous, Unbelievable, Charming, Loving, Attractive, Loud, Big, Proud, Fascinating, Managerial, Market-Driven, Masterful, Mature, Mechanical, Methodical, Modern, Moral, Motivated, Multilingual, Notable, Noteworthy, Objective, Observant, Opportunistic, Oratorical, Orderly, Organized, Outstanding, Participative, Participatory, Peerless, Perfectionist, Persevering, Persistent, Personable, Persuasive, Philosophical, Photogenic, Pioneering, Poised, Polished, Popular, Positive, Practical, Pragmatic, Precise, Preeminent, Prepared, Verbal, Victorious, Vigorous, Visionary, Vital, Vivacious, Well-Balanced, and No matter who you are...

FOREWORD

Marvin has written this book to let you all know that THERE IS A WINNER IN YOU! As a man of God that has experienced highs and lows he has learned to persevere through it all and channel the inner winner within himself to press on despite the odds. Through this book he wants to teach you all how to do the same thing and understand that no matter who you are or where you are from you are still a winner. His desire is for the message in this book to have a positive impact in your life and change the way you view your lows or times where you feel as though you are losing remembering that no matter what it looks like you are still a WINNER!

Marvin McQueen will take you step by step through this book teaching you how to change your way of thinking, become a more positive person and equip you to recognize your full potential.

Through real life experiences he will show you how to:

Wear a champion attitude
Inform yourself daily
Nurture the whole man (yourself)
Never give up
Empower yourself and
Reach

If you are willing to follow these guidelines you are well on your way to becoming the WINNER you were created to be! Marvin understands that life sometimes throws you curveballs but he has learned and wants to teach you that if you know who you are nothing is impossible. This book will encourage, uplift and bless your soul. It is going to totally transform the way you view you and think about life. I ask that as you read this book you open your mind to receive the inspiration to become the very best person that you can be.

Chrishaun Hollins

Let's take a journey to be a **WINNER**:

- Wear a Champion Attitude
- Inform Yourself Daily
- Nurture the Whole Man
- Never Give Up
- Empower Yourself
- Reach and Responsibility

Introduction

Introduction

The book you are about to explore is an uplifting tool and a push of encouragement to become a winner and to be a winner. Not just a winner but to understand that a winner is already inside of you. A winner is not about a win or loss column, it is not about you being undefeated, it is not about how many trophies you are holding on to, it is not about how many championship banners you have hanging in your home, or is it not about being called the most valuable player.

A winner or being a winner is a mindset on how to handle anything and everything in your life. No! You will not get it right every day, yet your mindset must be expanded to think before you act, think before you speak, and think before you say you have it under control. A winner lives their life and tries to find their place by not failing at the things they can control. This book will inform you, encourage you, shape you, and ultimately help change your mindset through reflecting on where you are now and where you can be if you put your mind to it.

Enter As You Are

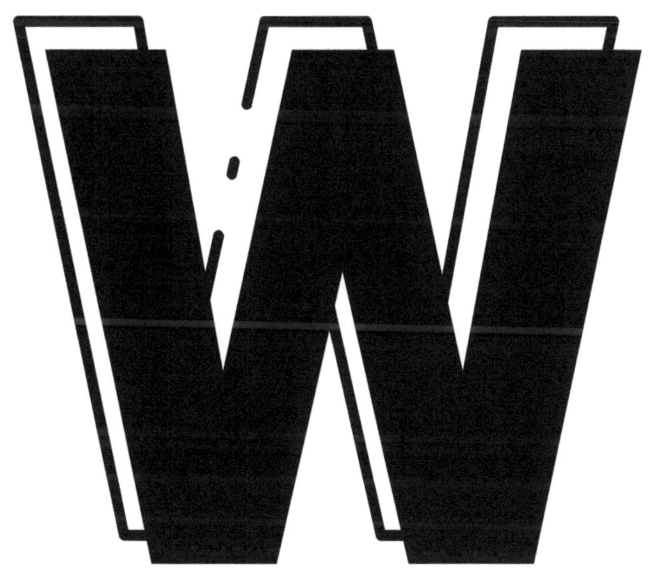

Wear a champion attitude

Wear a champion attitude

Today is a good day! Every day that we wake up is a good day. Each day we have routines, schedules, and agendas that must be handled to take care of the necessities of life. You wake up to brush your teeth, take a nice shower, make up your bed, and choose your clothes for the day.

Unfortunately, we all make the mistake of not being properly dressed for the day. The day that we face is the arena for where you will be placed on display. We are normally concerned about shoes, smell, and style. As those are important, we should remember to wear our attitudes. The attitude of an individual can be a factor of disposition, a state of mind, and a transition to be optimistic in body manner. Every day we wake up, it is a choice to take an opportunity to wear an article of clothing that shapes the schedule of the day. It is a garment of attitude that makes the best out of our agendas and routines. A great way to think of an attitude is that shirt that covers your body, which holds the inner most feelings that nobody should see on you.

Your attitude is the key to your development and progress in life. Often times, we want to be successful, yet our attitudes are on the incorrect frequency of where our lives need to be. Your attitude is a part of your wardrobe. The attitude is not just an accessory that should be taken any kind of way, but it should have a strong adjective to best describe where an individual is headed in life. We display our attitudes based on where we are currently, and it is a sad indication that we would rather stay there and struggle instead of moving forward.

A Champion = A Winner

What is a champion?

A champion is the one that is the victor at the end of a competition, struggle, or contest. There are many definitions and mental input of a champion. I want to place an extra effort on what we should think about a champion. A champion is a winner. A champion is positive. A champion is the greatest. A champion is a participant. A champion wants more.

A champion is a dreamer. A champion can be described however you feel personally. We must learn to choose to be a champion.

Life gives us choices to be whatever we want to be. If you plan, prepare, and position yourself correctly the sky is the limit. I want to encourage you that you can do what you put your mind to at any given time. Your mind and your view of things dictate what you will accomplish in your life. Your desire, thinking, and your attitude increases you to be that champion you aim to become. You will not win everything, but you can make it out with another experience that builds the champion in you. As we want to be champions or desire to be champions, we should have the attitude of a champion.

What is the attitude of a champion?

First, an attitude is the manner of disposition or the product of how they act because of certain situations.

Attitudes are sometimes relative to what life, work, or relationships bring to us. The attitude of a champion is above the average attitude of most people. Most people think wrong, therefore their actions are wrong. We all must think in the direction where our life is going. Most people take their first thoughts at the sign of adversity as negative, ready to give up, just go through without a care, or with no control of themselves. You are fortunate at this time to know that your attitude can be effective to where you are and where you are going in life. The attitude of a champion must push to excellence, strive for success, and want to excel in anything. Now I do not want to confuse anyone, or have you interpreted this attitude as having to be first in everything, yet you should be able to handle and control what you can. It is not about being undefeated, but it is about handling or taking on circumstances where your attitude is displayed as positive. Whether something good or bad happens, you can think and know that there will be an opportunity for you to seize. The attitude of a champion knows that a winner is on the inside of them.

Let's Talk It Out

Do you want to be a champion?

What is your attitude about yourself? Life? Goals?

Name one thing you can use in your personal life from wearing a champion attitude.

Inform Yourself Daily

Inform Yourself Daily

Inform yourself daily means that we should gain information to use every day in life. As a person or individual, we live because of information, and it can be transformed to wisdom and understanding.

What is Information?

Information is simply knowledge received. Information can be gained through a wealth of channels; Channels such as research, magazine, books, and people around the world. Information runs this entire world. If we turn on our televisions or pick up our cell phone, there is information staring in the face, we have to gather information, and place it in the relevant places or spaces of everybody life. Many people would tell you that a wealthy amount of information is good for you.
Even though I agree, I must take it further and remix it. Gain knowledge and use what you have received to progress daily.

Information is power and ammunition. When there are times of conflict, you will need information to remove the conflict.
Whenever things are not running as smooth as they should, it is called conflict. Unfortunately, as long as we live there will
be all types and all levels of conflict. Once you have the power, ammunition that is, you will be able to use it.., reload.., use it again..,reload.., every single day.

How to inform yourself?

Inform means to supply yourself with knowledge. Informing is a good task for us to remember when, how, and what to feed yourself or give yourself. When I think of the phrase "inform yourself", I am reminded of an older activity game called MEMORY. MEMORY was a game that had picture cards in a box. The picture cards were to be turned over where the players cannot see the face of the cards. The memory game objective is to match the information of two different cards that display the exact thing. As the cards were turned over, you could pick and choose any card to turn face up as long as it matched another card to make a pair. Sometimes in life, we are living like the memory game. As we move around daily, we may have collected many cards of information, yet we must use each card to match the times of our life. Once we have obtained matches, you must understand the match.

Matching information means to make sure things are alike and can be viewed exactly the same in a mirrored situation. As the world turns and goes through a repetitive pattern there's nothing new that is happening that hasn't happened before.

History is the product or intersection of experience and information. My father taught me to observe, not judge what people go through because that's your history lesson of what happens when a certain decision is made.... Now, that's information!

Let’s Talk It Out

Explain a good day for you.

How do you know what is good or bad information?

Name one thing you can use in your personal life from informing yourself daily?

____

____

____

____

____

____

____

____

____

____

____

Nurture the Whole Man

Nurture the whole man (yourself)

To be all you can be, there must be nurturing. Nurturing means to take care of yourself or something that you feel is valuable. Nurturing is that second nature when you are ready to feed and protect. To nurture the whole man means to take action in improving, progressing, training, and encouraging yourself because there is a priceless value within you. You have to make a decision to want what is best for you. Nobody can make a choice for you; it is up to you to choose what you want out of your life. We should never let ourselves be without care and protection from things that will hurt us in the short periods or long periods of our existence. One choice can affect your life for the good or the bad. Choices to nurture yourself can send elevate your life or it can push you downhill.

How do I nurture myself?

Just as a mother nurtures their child, we can do that internally with and without our parents.

You must make a smart choice and give yourself the best, even if you are still searching for the best. Life is a process that contains development through the improving times and discipline. One should learn about them to find out what disciplines and improvement is needed.

Please don't be sensitive to knowledge and think you have it all together. One of the first things you must realize that you can be better. Encourage yourself, get to know you, spend time thinking to yourself, question how, when, where, and why to yourself, and develop the nurturing component to take care of everything about you. You need exercise physically, mentally, and socially. You need nutrients to fight off unhealthy things that will contribute to the tearing down of your body. You need vitamins to help increase energy, strengthen bones, and help maintain blood flow throughout your body.
We must never forget to nurture, protect, and love you.

NURTURE SUGGESTIONS:

1) Get some good rest and relaxation

2) Exercise daily (no matter the timeframe)

3) Hang out with positive people

4) Eat healthy

5) Train your mind not to worry

6) Work what you have until you get what you want

7) Love, Live, and Laugh as much as you can

8) Love yourself

Let's Talk It Out

What steps do you use now to build yourself?

How do you choose the right things to help build your life?

Name one thing you can use in your personal life from nurturing the whole man?

____

____

____

____

____

____

____

____

____

____

____

Never Give Up

Never give up
Never give up (repeat it!)

Never give up means do not stop trying to do better. Make sure you never say that you can't do it, say it, and you got to - have to believe it.

Today, you can make it. Life has its share of successes and failures, and they work out to be the catalyst to change your life. To never give up is to never cease your dreams. In other words, do not stop dreaming. Dreams come from determination and sincere perseverance. Dreams come in different sizes and packages. Dreams can be general and personal. In a general sense, one person can dream and hope for something great for a whole nation. The thought of one person can help them go forward or hurt them into going backward. It is good to have a mind to progress not regress. Our society, cultures, and traditions have made an illegal training session on our decisions of life. The illegal training session says if you don't (do not) make it at first, then its not meant for you.

I beg to differ because there are multiple ways of reaching goals but you can not ever give up. In life, there are opportunities that we hit or miss, but the opportunities are given to you to make something of you. Please do not have something given to you, and you give it up. You were given a chance to live; now it's your turn to take that chance.

Thoughts and Quotes to Never Give Up

"Our greatest glory is in never failing, but in rising every time we fail."
- Ralph Waldo Emerson

"A limit on what you will do puts a limit on what you can do."
- Anonymous

"Many of life's failures are people who did not realize how close they were to success when they gave up."
- Thomas Alva Edison

"Never give in, never give in, never; never; never; never - in nothing, great or small, large or petty - never give in except to continuous of honor and good sense.
- Winston Churchill

"You just can't beat the person who never gives up."
- Babe Ruth

"So we must not get tired of doing good, for we will reap at the proper time if we don't give up"
- Galatians 6:9

"Never let your head hang down. Never give up and sit down and grieve. Find another way."
- Satchel Paige

"Don't give up trying to find our way. But remember that sometimes it takes bending to avoid breaking.
-Katinka Hesselink

"I look up to the hills, but where does my help come from? My help comes from the Lord, who made heaven and earth"
Psalms 121:1-2 (NCV)

"In everything we have won more than a victory because of Christ who loves us"
- Romans 8:37 (CEV)

Let's Talk It Out

Do you want to be better? Why?

How do you choose the right things to help you never give up when life gets hard?

Name one thing you can use in your personal life from never give up?

___

___

___

___

___

___

___

___

___

___

___

Empower Yourself

Empower Yourself

Empower yourself means to believe in you and your growth. You are a great person of great character that must make it to your full potential. I found myself trying to figure out why was everyone using the big words of empower, empowering, and empowerment.

As I read dictionaries, mission statements of corporations and poems, these words carry weight to them. I do not want you to use any words to sound better or as if you want to feel important, yet use words that can be used due to the full understanding of the words. The word empower (dictionary.com) is to give power or authority to, to enable or to permit, and to authorize by legal or official means. You have the privilege and ability to empower yourself in life.

For an example, a house is a fortress of ideas, blueprints, designs, art, furniture, appliances, concrete, brick and martyr, grass, glass, insulation and drywall. These things that I named may not be half of what goes into the construction of a house.

There is one more important item that really puts this house puzzle together.... What is it? .....Electricity. Electricity is the power, lights, and water in the house. Without the power, the home or house is just a structure. Can I get real with you? Of course I can! If you do not have some portion of power, you are just a structure. You were not placed on earth to dwell, you are here to live. The world is alive, and it is necessary to have alive elements in the world. In order for you to be more than a human being, you must be a human doing. You do base on what you believe in. Ask yourself, what do I believe in? It is not a complicated question and answer; it is dependent on your actions.

You have to believe in YOU! Say this: “I believe in ME.” I tell myself this a few times a week because I’m in constant daily growth. Life may not be easy, yet it is worth it. Set life by what you believe. Believe in what works for you. Believe in the standards that will empower you to become better, stronger, brilliant, smarter, wiser, and responsible. Until you are connected with power and believe, you will not be what you are really capable of.

Let’s Talk It Out

1) Point out areas where you find that it is hard to believe in yourself.
Why is it hard to believe?

Keys to Empower Yourself

Make up your mind to become better!

Step out from where you are now!

Throw out old bad habits!

Pray and Read the Word of God!

Change!

Be determined!

Associate with others that are going somewhere in life!

These keys to empowerment are a few steps and principles you can use in your life. You can add to these principles and make it work just for you. You are the only one that can change you.

Reach and Responsibility

Reach and Responsibility

When I was a little boy, there was a game I played with my father where he would pick me up and let me hold on to the playground monkey bars. Now, I must tell you that it was in our imagination. The playground monkey bars were our clothes line. Don't laugh because I know that most of you remember these games of our imagination. The objective of the game was to see how long can I hold on and not drop down to the ground or not let go. My dad would ask me, "Are you ready?" I would start laughing immediately and respond "Yes Sir!" He comes up to me, then and says "Reach.... Get on your tippy toes.... Jump and reach for it." With a huge smile and boyish giggle, I do it with his help. While hanging there, my arms and body are stretching. I look around, look down, arms are getting a little tired, legs are hanging and dangling, and now I'm looking to the ground ready to let go. A few seconds later I let go and dropped down to the ground. I was so excited because I was able to reach for something that was higher than I was just by my dad's help.

Everyone should understand that you should want to reach up for higher things in life. If you notice, we all want better things in life. Well I am not trying to think for you, just letting you know that you can get better and go higher in your life. All we have to do is reach for wherever you want to go or be in life. The direction you stretch to focus on the negative elements of life, you will become a negative person. It is issues, problems, and burdens that we spend more time on. Listen, everyone has made mistakes, everyone has been upset with decisions made in life, family may not love you as you want them to, your marriage may not be what you trusted it to be, your job may not be the best career, your house may not be your dream home, but you must reach for more.

REACH IS YOUR RESPONSIBILITY

You are able to reach any heights if you take on the responsibility to reach for it.

Responsibility

When I was about 10 yrs old, my parents afforded me the opportunity of have a very important responsibility. One of my first responsible jobs was keys to the house and I was very happy yet nervous. I was happy because my parents trusted me with the keys, yet nervous because I did not want to lose the keys and disappoint my parents. Getting the keys to the house was my opportunity to show how responsible I can be as I was growing up. If I can be trusted with these keys, then I can be trusted with more. A winner's life progresses through the things they can handle with care.

Responsibility is the key in making yourself out to be a great person, not only a great person, but a winner. Responsibility is that one thing that will be the discipline to you becoming what you want to become.

Even if you have made any mistakes, responsibility can bring you or put you back on track. Responsibility makes you successful.

As our lives grow, we find out that things come to us automatically. We may not necessarily want to pick up responsibility, but life grows within us and it happens. When you are a child, you were accountable to act like or take care of child things. Your child responsibility was to play, grow, eat, be loved, play, and want toys. Once you moved to Kindergarten and grade level age, the responsible thing was to act like a child get good grades, go to school and represent mom and dad, then come home to be rewarded for being a good child. Often times, people down play their childhood, but childhood is a good starting foundation for shaping our adulthood. Out of all the responsibilities we currently have, I want to add one more to your list. This responsibility is called be a winner. You are a winner because there is a duty you have to never give up. There is a great responsibility that will help you become the winner that you are. I want to encourage you to live your dreams and change your reality. You have the challenge, power, and privilege to take control of your life. No matter if your reality is poor or low, you can create a standard and way to live over your circumstances.

No matter if you have lost your job, house, friends, or cars, you can bounce back. Failing is not final. Losing things does not make you a loser. Stress does not take away success. A stumbling block does not mean stop. It's your responsibility, your ability, and your mind to own, to take control and rise up and be a winner.

things to know about a WINNER

10) One that believes that the sky is the limit
9) One that is real
8) One that is blessed
7) One that wants a fresh start
6) One that is true to one self
5) One that wants more and more
4) One that refuses to quit
3) One that has a mindset of victory
2) One that faces problems and troubles
1) A person like you

Echoes of A Winner

What is A Winner?

"It is one that keeps striving despite opposition! Rather you finish first or last as long as you finish, you are a WINNER!"
N. Canady, Atlanta, GA

"Someone who gives there ALL, no matter what the outcome is!"
P. Simmons, Jacksonville, FL

"A winner to me is someone that has love, health, family, close friends, and a good spiritual foundation in your life! With those things you have everything you need and that qualifies you as being a WINNER!"
R. Meadows, Orlando, FL

"The one who finishes first, the one who doesn't necessarily finish first, yet still finishes, the one who overcame the most obstacles and STILL finishes the race in spite of them, and the person who finished a race will become if he or she trains, studies the craft of the race, and tries again.
S. Gregory, Tallahassee, FL

Welcome to the Winner's Circle!
For more information and resources, visit
www.marvinmcqueen2.com

www.ingramcontent.com/pod-product-compliance
Ingram Content Group UK Ltd.
Pitfield, Milton Keynes, MK11 3LW, UK
UKHW021051270726
13967UKWH00012B/319